It's Ok, I'm All Right

How?

JEAN BROWN

WESTBOW
PRESS®
A DIVISION OF THOMAS NELSON
& ZONDERVAN

WestBow Press books may be ordered through booksellers or by contacting:

WestBow Press
A Division of Thomas Nelson & Zondervan
1663 Liberty Drive
Bloomington, IN 47403
www.westbowpress.com
1 (866) 928-1240

Editor:
Dr. Donna J. Gray
Professor
Trevecca Nazarene University

Scripture quotations taken from The Holy Bible, New International Version® NIV® Copyright © 1973 1978 1984 2011 by Biblica, Inc. TM. Used by permission. All rights reserved worldwide.

ISBN: 978-1-9736-8678-1 (sc)
ISBN: 978-1-9736-8677-4 (e)

Print information available on the last page.

WestBow Press rev. date: 2/25/2020

This is dedicated to my loving husband, my family, and my friends who were there with me over these past sixty-seven years of my life. And to everyone who said, "You ought to write a book." I finally got it written.

Contents

Preface

I wrote my life story because people who know me and those whom I have encountered in years of ministry have told me frequently through the years "You need to write your story." At the time they told me that, I just didn't have the time to write. And, even though I wrote many papers for undergraduate and graduate school, I didn't consider myself a writer. I was a pastor's wife, mother, graduate school student, and special education teacher.

A time came a few years later when cancer slowed me down. I was so glad that God had impressed me to take out short-term disability insurance at the beginning of the school year. It allowed me to take leave from teaching. In the past we were with individuals from church and family members who underwent chemo treatments. I knew the effects of those treatments were hard on the body. At this time, my husband's career had changed: Alongside being an interim pastor, he was a professor. Surprisingly, I actually felt like writing on the days that I had enough energy.

I thought my story would be complete following the cancer, but even more happened in my life after the cancer. At that point I looked into the future with these words on my heart and my mind: "It's okay, I'm all right". But how could those words be true? It is my desire that all who read my story will feel encouraged in their journey in life. Life has brought many surprises my way; some have been good and some were not. They were difficult. It's okay, I'm all right.

Jean Brown

Foreword by K. Brown

The seasons of the years teach lessons for life. Winter was enjoyable in childhood. Cold and snow often meant a break from school and playtime fun. Summer was freedom. The school year was over and life was relaxed as each day was savored; warmth permeated life.

Adulthood brought a different perspective to seasons. The weight of maturity brought difficulty and discomfort to wintertime. The cold bit the adult (harder). Winter weather made the days more difficult and complicated.

Summer was no longer freedom as in the adolescent sense, yet it carried different meaning. The flow of seasons parallels the flow of life. There are those seasons in which life has the exuberance of summer. The spirit is high; circumstances proceed smoothly. But those highs are countered by the lows and cold of life's winters. The events of life proceed like a bumpy country lane. Cold winds blow from the presence of people with whom we deal. At times, winter's blast is nearly enough to bring us down.

Emerson, however, knew correctly: "The years teach much which the days [and seasons] never know." True enough, we've tested and learned from those years. Winter, no matter how brutal its grip, need never be the final word. There will still be life's ice and cold, but there is one who, in its midst, brings summertime to the heart. That one is the friend closer than a brother, Jesus the Lord.

Introduction

Sing joyfully to the Lord, you righteous;
it is fitting for the upright to praise him.
Praise the Lord with the harp;
make music to him on the ten-stringed lyre.
Sing to him a new song;
play skillfully, and shout for joy.
For the word of the Lord is right and true;
he is faithful in all he does.
The Lord loves righteousness and justice;
the earth is full of his unfailing love.
Psalm 33:1-5 NIV

My husband and I started on a journey that took us three times into graduate school, seven full-time pastoral assignments, and seven interim pastoral assignments over a forty-three year period, in addition to twenty-eight years of full-time teaching for me and an eventual medical retirement. As we moved, God provided teaching positions for me. I was a special education teacher for most of those years. That role was not a part of my plans when I left college, but it was providential in God's plans for my life as I enjoyed working in that field of teaching. To add to our responsibilities, God gave us a son and a daughter to parent.

Each season can symbolize a period of time in human lives. Summertime, for instance, really does represent times of reprieve, regrouping, restoration, reassurances, and times of gathering resources. But can we have summertime in our daily lives when feelings of discouragement, disappointment, and despondency impact us? Can we really say, "It's okay, I'm all right"?

CHAPTER 1
God's Resources Revealed through Wisdom and Knowledge

At the age of 54, I heard words that could have frozen my spirit. A CT scan revealed that a mass attached to my thymus gland was lying against my aorta and against my pulmonary arteries. I didn't know anything about the thymus gland. I did not take biology in high school. Instead, I took chemistry, for I had no interest in learning anything about the bones, muscles, or glands in the body. So, when I sat down with the surgeon to discuss the surgery, he had to show me the CT scan pictures. He told me that he could not remove the tumor from the throat area. The only option I had was to undergo surgery similar to open-heart surgery. My sternum had to be separated to get to the mass. Do you know anyone who would look forward to that type of surgery? I was not at all excited. In fact, I had hoped never to have that type of procedure. I have family members who have had to undergo open-heart surgery. Thus, I was not standing in line waiting for this like those who wait in line for Early Bird sales over the Thanksgiving holidays.

But I knew something wasn't physically right. I was running low on energy levels beyond what I knew as normal, and I was having difficulty swallowing. Plus, I found it difficult to catch my breath. Because of feeling pressure and heartburn, I had to take up to four antacids at a time. I had been going to the doctor, who ran tests.

The tests kept coming back negative. The doctors weren't finding anything wrong. My only hope was to go to God in prayer. I asked Him to help me find the answer. A week later I was teaching reading skills to a group of my students when I began to have pains that resembled blood clots in the lung (a previous experience) or pains that could be associated with a heart attack. I called my doctor's office, and the receptionist told me that the nurse suggested that I go to the ER. So, like any good patient, I checked out in the school office and drove myself to the ER. On the way I asked God to help me get to the ER without having a massive heart attack. At some point God must have thought, "Sometimes you expect me to stretch your guardian angels."

Most people would have gotten a ride to the ER or called an ambulance. I did leave a message on my husband's cell phone and left a message for him at work. (Not exactly the best way to inform your husband you are driving yourself to the ER and it might be a heart attack). I told the physician assistant (PA) that I had experienced blood clots before, so, the PA in the ER ordered a CT scan because my EKG was normal. God used the information I shared from my past physical experiences with blood clots to help the physicians find the major problem; otherwise, they might have sent me home. The PA listened to me. He offered to run a CT scan even though the blood work came back negative for blood clots. He believed me that something was wrong. (God's resources, the right person at the right time.) He used the medical field's knowledge that he had granted. Because the results showed a tumor, the surgeon referred me to a surgeon. After talking to the surgeon, my husband and I found out that ninety percent of these types of tumors are benign. That was going to be me, right? After all, my small group at church prayed for me, and I was anointed by the pastor. We were following the biblical example for healing. I even told my principal and my students at school that I would be back in a couple of weeks after Christmas break.

That was not to be the case, though. When I awoke from the

surgery, my husband's words were, "It was malignant." My husband was very concerned but tried not to show feelings of despondency. I wasn't able to respond with my voice, being still on systems used after open-heart surgery, but I was able to write. It took my family a few minutes, but they finally figured out my sign language. I wanted to write something. I penned these words: "It's okay, I'm all right." All right?? I had just been told that I had a large cancerous mass they removed. Maybe I responded that way because I was still on heavy medication? No, I knew with confidence that if God helped me find my physical problem, He could help me through this. Our son leaned over and told me, "The God who brought me back from Iraq twice is the God who will get you through this."

My dependence on God would be a part of the solution. Some would ask, "Why was there a malignant tumor? After all, you followed through with anointing and prayer. Had God ignored your prayer?" No, I trust His providence, however it comes into my life. God was going to use the doctors' knowledge and chemotherapy to rid my body of the cancer. I claimed the verses found in Psalm 34:1-4:

> I will extol the Lord at all times; his praise will always be on my lips.
>
> My soul will boast in the Lord; let the afflicted hear and rejoice.
>
> Glorify the Lord with me; let us exalt his name together.
>
> I sought the Lord, and he answered me; he delivered me from all my fears. (NIV)

CHAPTER 2
God's Reassurance in Unexpected Situations

I went into that surgery with a calm that I did not have with any of the six other surgeries that I had been through, including a ten-day stay in the hospital for having multiple blood clots in both my lungs. I had asked God to help the medical team select the best surgeon for my situation. Of course, I also asked God to guide his hands.

Little did I know just how important that prayer would be. The surgery took five hours; it was predicted to last from one to three hours. The surgeon sent his nurse to tell my family about the tumor. It was 8" wide, and it had grown into the protective sack of my heart. It had wrapped itself around the nerves for my vocal chords and my nerves controlling my left shoulder and arm. It had affected my left lung, too. I was given three units of blood. The nurse told the family, "I'm sorry."

My family believed that apparently the medical people on the surgery team believed I wouldn't come through the surgery. The tumor stretched all the way through my chest cavity and was putting pressure on my esophagus and my stomach. The surgeon had to cut the tumor away from the nerves for my vocal chords, my shoulder, and my arm. He wanted the family to know that I could wake up with paralyzed vocal chords or problems with my shoulder and arm. Perhaps we were in a fight for my life as it had existed. If I kept my voice, I could audibly praise the Lord. If I kept my voice, I could continue teaching special needs children. If my heart would remain strong, then I would be left here on earth for some more time. In my opinion, Satan would not like for me to have any means of sharing God's grace and mercy using my voice. All of that depended on the outcome of the surgery. Naturally, my family went to prayer. My husband, my son and his family, my daughter and her family, my mom, and my middle sister were there. Our pastor was present to lead them in the prayer. And I know they continued to pray without ceasing until I awoke in the recovery room.

A day later they removed the tubes from my mouth: I was able to speak. What a miracle! What an answer to prayer! Although we tease each other about the fact that perhaps a few days without a voice would have given my husband and family a "little relief." My husband told me that my being quiet would've been a special treat, but only for a few days; he knew that would bring about a smile. God protected my vocal chords. He knows me well. Being without a voice is one thing that might have been more than I could bear at the time. Praising God with my voice means so much to me. I have sung solos and duets, sung in the choir, and led music in the church. Twelve and half years after the surgery, I still have full use of my voice. God knew His plan for me would include a larger ministry that would involve my using my voice.

My left lung atrophied, but I had 95% or greater oxygen intake. I am so thankful because over the years anytime I have to have a mask placed on my face I have a "mini" panic attack worrying about whether I will have enough oxygen to breath. I know that may seem foolish, but, growing up with asthma, I care about my oxygen intake. So, even though I had little concerns about the surgery, God made sure about the oxygen intake.

When I went into surgery, I had no idea what they would find. God did. He used a skilled surgeon. He guided his hands. I am also very grateful for the anesthesia that I got during surgery. I can't imagine how I as a patient would feel if I could hear the conversations that take place during surgery. I'm very glad that I did not know how quickly the tumor had grown, and I know the surgeon was surprised.

The first part of the journey led into the next part of the journey, which took six months of my time in chemotherapy for cancer. Each session lasted six and a half hours. I teased the nurses that I must be paying rent in here because everyone else leaves after two or three hours. I was usually their last patient of the day. They had to use the strongest chemo available because the cancer was very aggressive and it was in stage four. I had to sign papers concerning the most aggressive drug used in my particular case. Part of the paperwork included a statement that one of the chemo meds, referred to as "Dr. Red," could increase my heart rate and even cause my heart to enlarge. I could choose to use chemo with a chance that it would eliminate the cancer cells, or I was at liberty to choose to do nothing. It was a risk either way.

I chose the use of chemo knowing there were side effects. I believed in giving medical science a try since God had found doctors that I believed held the answers. I knew going in that the chemo might not work. But, I wanted to give it a try because I had too many reasons to hold on to life. I have been on the journey with Christ as my Lord and Savior for sixty-one years. At the time that I was going through the chemo, I had been a Christian for forty-eight years. Being a Christian had taught me that God is there to bring about victory through life's problems. It is His presence that brings sunshine during those cold wintry times in our lives.

Had my journey prior to cancer been easy? No, so how did I reach the place of saying, "It's okay, I'm all right"? How can I smile each day? Each day we awake is a new day for each of us. Some would ask, "Why did you make it, and some did not?" Only God has the answer to that question. There are days when I wonder that same thing. A young mother who was taking chemo at the same time that I did, did not make it. In our years of ministry, we have seen some people live through some rough physical issues and others who did not make it. My only thoughts were, "I am ok, and I am alright because I know my creator and He knows me. I have His assurance through it all." My prayers have always been that those who left this world earlier than I had that same reassurance at the end of their lives.

This is our story. We are still on the journey.

Deuteronomy 31:6 (NIV) says it best:

> "Be strong and courageous. Do not be afraid or terrified because of them, for the Lord your God goes with you; he will not never leave you or forsake you."
>
> "Do not be afraid...of them," then, doesn't just mean people; the word "them" could represent things in our future. He will not fail nor forsake.

CHAPTER 3
God's Resource/Special Gift

As I mentioned in the earlier chapter, I became a Christian at age six. My thirst for knowing Jesus first began as a young child. My mother sang to me when she rocked me to sleep, and she always sang about Jesus. There was a joy that came through those songs. From that, I knew Jesus was special. I also heard her speak His name in prayer. I can't thank God enough for allowing me to be born into her family. My mother knew she was having difficulty in her pregnancy, even though she didn't comprehend it all at the time. She and my dad were living on an army base in Alaska. She told God that she would dedicate the child to His Kingdom if the child lived. She never saw the same doctor twice. I was born prematurely.

Knowing what I know as a special education educator, I am amazed that I am alive today. I am even more amazed that I had any capacity for learning, although there are times when my family has teased me by saying that I taught special education so long that I became "special." God granted my mother's request. I was born in 1951 when there wasn't much research being done concerning premature babies. Neither my mom nor I knew the journey I would take, but she knew that dedicating me to God would serve as an open invitation for Him to be the guiding factor in our lives. We almost froze to death the winter after my birth. We lived in a small trailer house. The heat went out, and my dad was not easily reached, so she heated an iron on the stove, wrapped it in towels, and put it in bed with us to generate heat. (This, of course, was during a time when electric irons were not readily available – it was the real old-fashioned kind like you sometimes see on TV or in movies…kind of like cast iron). ☺

Reflecting on those very early days in my life, I realize that my mom laid the foundation for my faith. I am drawn to II Timothy 1:5 as found in the NIV:

> "I have been reminded of your sincere faith, which first lived in your grandmother Lois and in your mother Eunice and, I am persuaded, now lives in you also."

Timothy was blessed with a mother and a grandmother who helped him understand faith. Similar to Timothy's mother and grandmother, my mom wanted her children to have the same opportunity. God had been her sustaining strength through many experiences. She desired to see other generations in her family experience that same faith.

My mother knew the call of Jeremiah could also be my call: "Before I formed you in the womb I knew you, before you were born I set you apart" (1:5 NIV).

God knows all about us. What are you set apart for?

CHAPTER 4
God's Restoration Through Healing

The first summer that I can recall staying with my grandparents was quite a summer. Not only did I become a Christian at age six, but also I was a recipient of my grandmother's prayer for healing. I woke up in the middle of the night with a terrible earache. This was over six decades ago when there weren't convenience stores or Walmart stores that are open for twenty-four hours in which medicine was available for ear aches. My grandmother turned to the only source she knew. She asked me if I believed that God could heal my earache. My simple answer was, "If you believe He can, then I do, too." She put her hand on my ear and prayed for healing. The pain went away, and my ear was restored to hearing without pain.

This was one of those situations when we could call on God for healing without being at a church service. There were no elders present to anoint with oil. My grandmother had a lot of faith in God, and I can remember her faith as if it were yesterday. After she touched my ear and prayed for me, the pain was gone! God took over. What could have been a period of despondency turned out to be the beginning of my walking in faith. Not only did I believe in my grandmother's faith, but also I trusted God to heal my earache. As we all know, earaches can be very miserable. I experienced instantaneous healing. It helped me to understand that healing is possible with God. Later on I would learn how he also chooses to use the knowledge of medical science to assist in healing here on earth.

Wow, what a step of faith. That same summer my grandparents changed churches and began to attend the church where I became a Christian. It was just a block from where they lived. I remember becoming a Christian while I attended that Vacation Bible School. I asked Jesus to forgive me of my sins. My grandmother took time to visit with the Vacation Bible School teachers. They asked her if she thought that I could memorize Psalm 100 for the Vacation Bible School program. My grandmother proudly said, "Yes." When I had a chance to see how long it was, I wondered about my ability to memorize it. But my grandmother had more confidence in me than I had. During the summer, I saw reflected in my grandmother her love for and confidence in me and her love of scriptures.

Every afternoon I would practice my scripture memorization with her. My grandmother had great respect for God's word, and learning that scripture helped me to appreciate God's word. It helped me to see that we can commit it to memory. We can call on God's word frequently, even if we do not have a bible with us. During the times that I attended that church, I learned to respect the testimonies of the adult leaders in that church. The years allowed me many opportunities to be under their leadership. They, too, taught me so much about the faithfulness of God and the promises in His word. Psalm 100 (NIV) reads:

> Make a joyful noise unto the Lord, all the earth.
> Worship the Lord with gladness;
> Come before him with joyful songs.
> Know that the Lord is God.
> It is he who made us, and not we are his;
> We are his people, the sheep of his pasture.
> Enter into his gates with thanksgiving,
> And his courts with praise:
> Give thanks to him and praise his name.
> For the Lord is good and his love endures forever;
> His faithfulness continues through all generations.

After I memorized that scripture as a child, I took it to heart. When I thought about the words, I knew once again that knowing God must be special. After all, we are encouraged to sing, we are encouraged to be thankful, and we are encouraged to enter into His courts with praise.

I heard and sang hymns about God and Jesus. Those words reminded me of the early melodies I heard at home. As my days turned to years, the words meant more and more to me. As a Christian, I have come through a few winters in my soul. My childhood years and my teen years allowed me time to read and study God's word without going through many spiritual valleys. I found His word full of truths and admonishments to those who followed Him.

These words laid a foundation of faith on which for me to rely. In Chapter 11 of Hebrews I counted 20 verses containing the words "by faith. . . ." The verses that began with "By faith, . . ." mentioned several saints who followed God through tough times. Life was not easy for them, but they lived life, experienced it, and went on. How? By living with the knowledge that God their creator would remain steadfast and be there with them.

Just as they experienced disappointments, we, too, experience disappointments. Did my becoming a Christian at age six automatically make me free from times of discouragement? Did it mean that I would not be disappointed? Did it mean that I would not become despondent?

CHAPTER 5
Another of God's Resources/The Bible

My becoming a Christian guaranteed me of only one thing; Christ would walk with me to help me. However, He would only help me as I allowed Him to help. He can only work where He is welcome.

As we go through various stages of our lives we experience disappointments. But under what circumstances do those disappointments come? By whose judgment calls are we judging the disappointments? As our lives progress into the adult years, there are so many things we encounter. The words "It's okay, I'm all right" are not necessarily appropriate for every situation.

As we read the New Testament, we become familiar with an individual impacted by God, someone who would be known for his missionary journeys. His name was Paul, formerly known as Saul, who persecuted Christians. He was radically changed by an encounter with the Lord. He would have been able to say, "It's okay, I'm all right," even though he found himself in jail in a dark dungeon. There wasn't much physical sunshine in his area, but he found a way to bring God's warmth to those who surrounded him. Paul's witness is found in Acts 20: 19-24 (NIV): "I served the Lord with great humility and with tears…However, I consider my life worth nothing to me, if only I may finish the race and complete the task the Lord Jesus has given me—the task of testifying to the gospel of God's grace."

CHAPTER 6
God's Restoration/Attitude Adjustments
Through Our Situations

According to biblical scriptures, the story of Paul's life revealed that he went through some very rough trials, yet he endured those by staying focused on the goal of serving Christ. I, like Paul, wanted to stay focused on serving Christ. As I entered my young adult years feeling pretty prepared for my future, I wanted to be someone who would succeed. I had goals in mind, and I was ready for the future. Or so I thought. I wanted to be a leader and a person who could be used to help others find Christ as Lord and Savior.

I considered myself a type-A personality. Over the years, I sought approval. I wanted to make sure that everyone was pleased with what I was doing. My father was the hardest to please. I perceived him as a perfectionist. By the time I was nine, my dad did not like my making a grade below C. That added to the stress I felt concerning perfection by his standards. I dreaded getting report cards. In many ways there was a sense of fear in our home, not just for me but for all of us. I could tell my dad lacked something. He was a hard worker and always provided for our family. I knew he loved us, but, for him, each day was a new day of unpredictability.

We enjoyed vacations together, going out to eat, visiting family from time to time, but something was missing in his life to give him peace. My dad had a respect for God and Jesus. He never objected

14 | Jean Brown

when we went to church and he didn't. He grew up going to church, but he had issues in his life that he had not surrendered to God, and he was holding back. Change from the inside out is not that easy if we aren't willing to admit we need to change. During my teen years, I was very tired of my dad's unpredictability. In fact, I complained to God about him. I especially complained at age fourteen. Wow, I'm glad God didn't strike me dead when I complained to him or give up on me at that point. God continued to tell me that I needed to love my dad and pray for him. I told God that I could pray for my dad's salvation, and I would try loving him. Over the period of four years, God softened my heart toward my dad. I began to see him based upon many things that fashioned my dad's life. I guess I was old enough to see him though God's eyes. My dad did give his life to God close to the end of my senior year of high school. He eventually became the president of his local Gideons. When he passed away in March of 2017 his dying words were, "It is well with my soul." I shudder to think what he might have said had I not been faithful to answer God's call to pray for my dad. God sometimes calls upon us to stand in the gap even for those whom it is not easy to forgive. I knew the scriptures taught us that Christ can forgive us only if we are willing to forgive others. My dad knew when he died that we loved him and God did, too. "It's ok, I'm alright" would be an appropriate phrase from me at that time. What peace and comfort we all had, knowing that my dad left this world to be in the presence of the Lord.

CHAPTER 7

God's Reassurance Through
His Second Work of Grace

When I was only twelve, when I found myself praying to God and asking Him to fill me with his Holy Spirit, to be empowered by Him. I wanted Jesus to be Lord of my life. The desire of my heart was to be the best Christian I could be. I was taught that God is perfect. We as Christians can seek to be more like Him. That is not a bad goal. However, it sometimes is a bad goal when Christians seek to fit an exact mold. This was one of my biggest struggles. With years of reading many inspirational books and many books written by missionaries, I felt prepared for my new journey. I continue to admire devoted servants of God. In my college years I had more unstructured time to read God's word. So, why wouldn't I be prepared? Utopia, right?

It was a good thing for me that the lives of those Christians who surrounded my life helped me to see that life isn't always Utopia. I thought if I did all the right things, as I understood them, life should be okay. (Deep in my heart I wasn't sure that I could always do the right things that would bring about perfection in every situation.) I had asked God to be Lord of my life at the age of twelve, and I accepted a call to full-time Christian service. I spent years preparing for the future. I learned through those years that only God could bring about the right ending to every situation. So many times we try to bring that about on our own. We just need to wait and trust His leadership, for only He has the answer. We must be willing and patient servants. James Chapter 5 reminds us of that truth – that waiting is tough to do in our society today. Nearly everything we do in life is based on results that are measured by man's approval. Norms that are established. Even when we prepare a meal, we listen for the words, "That tastes great."

I am blessed that one of the right things I did was to trust God to help me achieve the goal of attending a Christian college. My family had very little money to help with the cost of college. In fact, my father bought a boat before he gave his life to serving Christ. He told me that he used money he could have given me for college to buy his boat. I think my father used that as a means to challenge my dedication to God and the call I felt on my life. Knowing that was the situation, I sought God's help. I believed that God wanted me to teach students in elementary schools. At that time in my life I believed it would be children on a mission field. My family tried to convince me that I should attend a state college. I knew in my heart that God wanted me to attend a Christian university. I knew that I had a call to Christian service, and I could take more classes there to prepare me for that part of my life. I stepped out on faith believing God. He surprised me with His provisions through scholarships, grants, and loans. Part of those provisions included jobs that He also provided. I am a firm believer that if we are following the will of God, He will provide. I trust His promise as found in Luke 11:9: "So I say unto you: Ask and it will be given you; seek and you will find; knock and the door will be opened to you" (NIV).

As a teen and young adult, I struggled with this promise. I wondered if I lacked enough faith when some of those doors didn't open. Why were some doors opened and others that I wanted to open not opened? I can say with a calm assurance, Thank God, some of those did not open! God knew what was best.

CHAPTER 8

God's Resources in His Provisions/ Provision of a Christian Husband and Learning to Trust

The scripture does not say just how long it will take for the door to open. It does not say how long it will take to find what we are seeking. Patience is so very important as we trust God for His provision. He has the keys to the right doors, and He knows which things will benefit us the most.

One of my blessings in life is God's provision of a husband. I had to wait for the right person. There were many times that I cried myself to sleep in high school and in college. I was disappointed that I wasn't one of the lucky girls who were going on dates. I wasn't one of the girls who got engaged. Although I did have opportunities to go out on dates during my high school years, I was not willing to sacrifice my standards and give up on the goal I had in life in order to have a date every weekend. The few dates that I did have in college were with young men whom I knew were dedicated Christians. They have continued to serve God alongside their dedicated wives.

My call to full-time Christian service remained steady. I knew that, if I fulfilled that call, I had to make certain that the guy that I would spend the rest of my life with would also be called of God. On those evenings that I found myself in tears, I would begin to pray. I would also find solace by reading my Bible. I was able to face another day after my faith and trust in the Lord had been renewed. My thoughts are, "Thank God!" Had I not waited, I would have missed God's special gift. The summer after my sophomore year in college I sat down and had a conversation with God. The longer I served God, the more I realized just how much solace I received when having conversations with Him. I took a piece of white scrap paper and wrote down all the characteristics I would like to have in a husband. I am so glad God understands me. He might have thought the list a little humorous because He already knew my thoughts, but He didn't condemn me for writing the list. Instead, He honored it! I still have that list. I keep it in a scrapbook and have shared it with young ladies facing those same issues – date or wait for the right guy.

I met my husband, Ken, during my junior year of college. When I observed him, I realized with great joy that he met all of the things I had listed on that piece of paper. Some of those things weren't easy to fulfill. For example, he would play an instrument (he plays three), he would be tall (not too difficult, for I am only 4' 11"), he would love children, he would have dark hair,☺ he would probably wear glasses (don't know why I added that one), he would be a great preacher, and he would love God with all his heart. Those are just a few on the list that might have sounded funny. Most people would think so, but I wrote them down anyway.

We were both members of a traveling choir that raised money for mission projects. Our group was in charge of coordination and delivery of the entire service in the churches we visited. I had an opportunity to hear him preach. After hearing Ken's first message, I knew that God had answered my prayers. In fact, I was so certain that I poked a girl sitting next to me in the choir loft, and I whispered, "I'm going to marry that guy." Her response was, "You have not even gone on a date with him." She must have thought my words were pretty silly. My conversations with God were not in vain. Ken is 6' tall, he wears glasses and when we first met he had brown hair. ☺

By that time in my life, I had been a Christian for fourteen years. God had become my closest friend, and I had learned that God cared about every area of my life. I didn't take God's word for granted. Come unto me all you who are weary and burdened, and I will give you rest" as found in Matthew chapter 11. (How I qualified "burdened" at the time was dependent on the fact that, as a young lady in college, I was anxious.) Being married to the right person was very important to me, and I did not want to miss God's will for my life. I came later to realize that God's perfect will for my life included just the right man. That is why with confidence I could say that he was the one I was going to marry. And, sure enough, he was. My husband's strength and faith have assisted me in being able to say, "It's ok, and I'm all right." He is my best friend. We rely on each other every day, and I have no regrets.

Trusting in His provision for a Christian husband was one thing; however, having an ongoing trust in His provisions for life was another thing. I learned to have an attitude of trust.

Our first home was a duplex apartment in Kansas City where the Nazarene Seminary is located. Every year we truly lived by faith because our job situations changed more than once. My faith was tried during that time because there were 100 applicants for every teaching job. I substitute taught for one year and I sold Tupperware. I am not, nor have I ever been, a great salesperson. However, I made enough to buy our groceries. My husband worked in a bank as a teller. We needed more income, so, I went to work as a secretary/receptionist for University of Missouri Kansas City.

I knew at the time that being a secretary was not among my best professional skills. At times I wondered if I ever would have the opportunity to use the training I had received in college, but the job helped us keep food on the table and our bills paid. I came to a greater appreciation of those who have to clock in every day on their jobs. Ken and I also served as Children's pastors for a church in Kansas City, Kansas. We had 250 children attending our church, and we were in charge of training of the Children's church workers. Naturally, due to our job description, we also served as Children's church workers ourselves. Additionally, through a program called Caravans, we had 150 children on Wednesday nights. It was set up for children to learn more about the Bible, the church, and other practical things in order to earn badges. God showed me through Children's ministries that my skills in teaching were not to be used just in a public school setting. It was part of my call to full-time Christian ministry. It was during those times that God helped me to share my testimony with adults. I had a fear of failure in that area because I never was able to memorize any of the four- or ten-step programs for witnessing to adults. Perhaps this was one of the first times as an adult that I learned, "It's ok, I'm all right." I had surrendered all to God, including where He led us. We didn't have much at that time in our lives, but we continued to serve as stewards of our time, talents, and our financial tithe to the church. God provided. During those days, I experienced immediate healing again. I will never forget being healed as a child. I needed to call upon that experience to help me as a young adult.

When I went in for a check-up, the doctor told me he found a lump. He was concerned about it but wanted to wait a few weeks and see how it developed. Most doctors were not using mammograms on a regular basis at that particular time. During those days I was a part of a ladies' Bible study on our block. I asked them to pray for me. I was very concerned and couldn't figure out why this would be happening prior to our going into full-time ministry. But I had to yield it to God in the only way I knew – through prayer. One night I asked my husband to anoint me with oil and pray for me. Fortunately, we had some olive oil in the house. At the point at which he anointed me, I sensed a warmth go through my body, and I knew God had healed me. When I went to the doctor for the check-up six weeks later, he told me that there was no sign of that lump. Praise God!

CHAPTER 9

God's Regrouping/ Our Being Ready for Change

Five years after we were married, God blessed us with a son. We took Lamaze classes. We had been told that we were a perfect couple. Natural childbirth would go well, or so I thought. Only God could have predicted an emergency C-section, and that was one situation He didn't let us in on until the time. Was it ok, all right? In my preparation, I had dismissed C-section as an option. After all, we were prepared. Once again I can say, "Thank God for doctors who knew what to do." Our son would not have lived had I been able to have natural childbirth. God was in control.

That morning I had my mom, my grandmother and my husband there to hold my hand and go to prayer with me. We committed it into God's hands. My physician was away at a conference. The attending physician was a 70-year-old who told me he hadn't delivered a baby in a while, but I could trust him. What could we do but believe that God could use him. Naturally, I was a little nervous; actually, let's just say I was very nervous. The only surgery I had ever had was removal of wisdom teeth. Just knowing I had been prayed for by my family and many Christian friends helped me to calm down. We were blessed to have a healthy son born that day. So, in spite of an emergency C-section, I could say with confidence, "Thank God, it's okay, and everything is going to be all right."

Being a new mom and recovering from a C-section at the same time definitely had its moments. Thankfully, I had a husband who was very helpful and very patient. Remember, part of my list said, "he would love children."☺ When our daughter arrived 2 ½ years later, having a C-section delivery was not a tough alternative.

The years of parenting that followed brought a lot of challenges. We wanted to make sure that we were doing all the right things as parents. We enjoyed the dedication services for both of our children. Those services were only the beginning. Our prayers for our children's futures had just begun. We sought knowledge in what we believed were all the right places. For instance, I had graduated from college with a Bachelor of Science degree in Elementary Education. Therefore, I should know much about children. Right? I had opportunities to read books by Christian authors on parenting. These should have been easy years, right? Not exactly.

In parenting, not all of our decisions always turn out right. We make judgment calls based on what we understand at the time. As with every generation, new challenges surfaced. This has been especially true in the technological age. Taking a stand against what we perceived to be wrong did not always come easily. We did listen to a contemporary Christian music station. We wanted to know the music of our children's generation. To our surprise, we actually enjoyed some of their Christian music. We encouraged our children to use discretion when choosing music. We knew from our generation that certain lyrics from secular music are not uplifting. Our children grew up during the time of "rap" music and when the theory of "no absolutes" became popular.

We believed, and continue to believe, that it was vital to understand the generation of our children and of our grandchildren. We now have seven grandchildren. If we are informed, then we can make some effort at teaching truth versus untruth. However, implementing great parenting every minute of the day in just the right way doesn't always happen. Yet, in those times, there is a constant on which we can depend. God is there when we ask Him to be there. Somehow in His mercy and grace He can take situations and bring about peace. We did not want our children to grow up without a love and respect for God's word and His standards. The only way that our family survived those years was when God interceded, because there were times when I felt I had made a mess due to a poor judgment call. At those times, I had to ask our children to forgive me.

CHAPTER 10

God's Restoration/Through Forgiveness/Communicating

At those times of navigating change, God taught us many lessons, lessons of forgiveness and communication. The words, "I'm sorry, please forgive me" were a part of our vocabulary. We believe it is important for children to see that adults make mistakes. We believe that children also need to see that it is okay to make mistakes. Failures do not mean that everything is over. I am so thankful that, when I messed up, God answered my prayers. We made it through the teen years. We spent a lot of time communicating with our children. Without fail, we assured our children that, even when they were being oppositional, we still loved them. Over the years, the consequences of their behavior changed because the situations were different. One of my husband's favorite things to say was, "There a price to pay for everything you do in life. You must decide what price you are willing to pay." He followed it with, "Life is filled with little disappointments, and this is one of yours." We wanted our children to understand choices and consequences. How important it is to know that love and security exist in a family. We believed it was and continues to be a vital part of family life. Many times the last minutes of the evening were spent in talking and praying together. We wanted our children to grasp the concept that prayer was and is the most important part of serving God.

One of my fond memories is the time when our daughter, at age 3 ½, decided to take four dolls to church. I tried to talk her into bringing just one or two. Her reply was, "No, Mommy, they all need to go." Wow, she had caught on to how we looked at ministry. I was brought to tears at that moment. When we arrived at church, she sat them in the pew with her. When prayer time came, she took all four of her dolls to the altar for prayer. I certainly didn't want to stop her. I followed her down to the altar. She even wiped the imaginary tears from their eyes. That morning her dad had a tough time finishing the pastoral prayer. It was a precious sight. In my heart I was pleased to see her do that. I have heard and read that values are sometimes caught instead of taught. She had seen us praying at the altar, and she wanted to do so, too. She had observed just how important prayer is in the life of a Christian.

We need to communicate with God even though sometimes His part of the conversation might involve change. More importantly, God is the creator. He knows us well. I knew and trusted our children's creator. God saw the whole picture, and so many times His Holy Spirit led me to know how to pray. I didn't always get an immediate answer, but I had new insight as to what direction to go. The desire of our hearts was that our children would not grow up with bitterness towards God and the church. We wanted them to see God's goodness and blessings, to know that no matter where life took us, we would serve God.

We didn't want our children to make poor social choices. We read all the books we could find about teens and participated with our children in all the church camps. We made finances available so that they could be involved with all of the church youth activities. We even made sure that our children could have friends over to our home and hosted many of the youth activities. Everything should have gone well, right? Once again, just having the knowledge, keeping communication going, and opening our home for guests were not enough. I found myself on my knees in prayer many times. We did not possess all the knowledge to solve every problem our children experienced. There were still things both of them experienced that we had not expected.

We came to rely on God more and more, not to just give us wisdom, but to lead us in how to pray. For instance, how could I pray for my son when I knew that he had chosen the wrong school friends? I knew from meeting the friends that they might not be good influences on him. How could I continue to be a parent in that situation without driving my child away? When my heart was breaking, how should I have reacted? Who could I tell without it reflecting on my job as a "good parent"?

We had moved to New Mexico during the transition years for our son. He was in the last year of middle school, and he wanted friends like any teen would. There were a lot of teens in our church, so we thought he would be secure there. Within a year of moving there, he had expanded his social group.

Our enemy, Satan, knew quite well what he would like to see happen. He would like nothing better than to destroy our son, his parents, the family, and the ministry. Our son grew up inviting friends to church. Many times he was told, "You'll never get that person in church." He did get those people to attend church in spite of the fact that he wasn't totally dedicated to God at that time. And even though I disagreed with his being their friend, his getting them to church may have been the only time some of them ever went to church. He has the gift of evangelism. Satan was not at all happy about that aspect of our son's personality. He wanted to destroy him. Praise God that is not how our story ends. What I am about to share is a reflection of God's great grace and mercy.

At times I had to pray difficult prayers. I was so fearful of the direction that our son was going that I told God in prayer that I would be willing to face anything except death if it would help get our son on track. Before I knew it I found myself in a Critical Care Unit with multiple blood clots in both my lungs, and I was very sick. When I was admitted, though, I had no idea just how critical I was, but my son knew. When he came to visit me, he told me that he had prayed. He told me that he had asked God not to let me die. He continued to say that God told him, "Your mom is ready to meet me, should she die, but you aren't." Wow! In that time, could I say as I lay there on the edge of death, "It's ok, I'm all right"? Praise God, I could say that. It was an important factor in our son's future. Our son found time to pray. However, the enemy wasn't finished with his plans.

When our son was old enough to drive, we let him drive a rather large vehicle. If I remember right, he nicknamed it "the boat." It became a means of transportation for him and his friends. The transportation wasn't always used for good. Wanting to relate to peers can lead teens into poor choices, and there came a time that I prayed that he would get sick from drinking with his friends. They were not drinking Dr. Pepper or iced tea! He came home sick. In fact, he got so sick that he thought he was going to die. That stopped his desire to participate with his friends, but he didn't mind being a designated driver. So, there came a time when I asked God to allow the "boat" to be in a wreck. The conditions were that my son and everyone involved would be allowed to walk away. I know this may seem like a strange prayer, but I trusted God. Within a week, an older lady hit our son's car with her car. It totaled "the boat." Everyone involved was okay. Our son was finished with driving for a while. At a time when he was receptive, I shared my prayers with him. Today he reflects on those prayers as lessons in relationships. He saw the kind of relationship that I had with God, and he learned more about a merciful God who understood humanity.

CHAPTER 11
Trusting Reliance/When "It's Ok" Doesn't Fit/Believing in Redemption

A few years later those lessons would carry him all 480 days of surviving Iraq as a member of the 82nd Airborne and another year of duty in Iraq with the Big Red One Infantry. During those tough teen years, he continued to respect God. In a struggle to choose between God and man, he reached a place in the later part of those teen years when he asked God to forgive him.

Our daughter has always been a delight in how she approached life. As I wrote earlier, she came to respect prayer at an early age. She continues to have a tender heart. She spent a lot of years helping me with children's ministries on the local and district levels, especially in New Mexico. Working with those younger than herself is something that she enjoyed. She was a leader for the younger youth in our church. It was and continues to be one of her gifts.

However, Satan wanted to rob her of that gift. Relating to the younger youth did not fill all the gaps in her life. As with all teens, she felt a need to be accepted by her peers. Our daughter, blessed with a beautiful voice, was involved with her peers in her high school choir. We attended her concerts and helped with fundraisers.

As with her brother, we took her to all the local and district teen activities sponsored by the church. More than one of those activities included seminars on "True Love Waits." We knew that this issue was a prevalent one for her generation. We even took time to purchase a special "True Love Waits" ring of her choice. Our daughter's personality and features made her a very attractive young lady, although I don't know that she always believed that about herself.

As a parent, I believed we were doing everything we could to help our daughter. I prayed for her as I did for her brother. She should have made it through her teen years without a major problem, right? Well, I would say, not exactly. Somehow, we as parents want to believe that things we say and do will guide our children through the teen years without their making poor choices. But maybe, just maybe, some of our guiding could turn into manipulations. I know, as a Type A personality, I would like to have orchestrated our children's lives away from poor decisions. We can't be with them every minute of the day, so we have to come to a place of surrendering our children to God over and over again. And, now, I find myself placing our grandchildren in His hands.

We do have this promise that, "Greater is He that is in me than he that is in the world." I had to lean on that for our daughter, too. At age sixteen our daughter began dating a young man who was not a believer. She was determined that she would be able to get him to attend church. He never came to church. He was eighteen. He was a high school and community soccer star. We could see that he probably would not want to give up his lifestyle, but I was caught in the struggle. I found that my prayer time was not an easy one. We were so very busy during that time in our lives. I wanted to encourage our daughter in her effort to help this young man, and yet, deep down inside, I felt as if I wasn't really helping the situation.

The phrase, "it's okay, I'm all right" just didn't seem to fit this situation.

Our daughter became pregnant the spring of her junior year of high school.

She is a part of a generation that had many options concerning teen pregnancy.. Our daughter chose to give birth. We were pleased with her decision. It would mean a lot of changes in our lives but we were willing to accept those changes. We wanted what was best for our daughter and the unborn child. Prior to our daughter getting pregnant she had joined us in city-wide efforts to celebrate life. We were in support of those who chose to be pro life. She was taking responsibility for her choices. Long before the baby was born, she sought out God's redemption. She gave birth to a precious baby girl during her senior year in high school. Our granddaughter was born on Thanksgiving Day. In many respects I would say, "how appropriate." We did give thanks that a healthy baby girl had been born.

George Barna's research group out of California conducted a study that showed that teen girls who participated in "True Love Waits" had higher pregnancy rates than non-participating teens. The research indicated that teens who participated in "True Love Waits" found themselves in situations without protection because the girls are also a part of a group that do not take birth control pills or have abortions. My husband and I came across that information a few years ago. We did not have that information when we were going through this with our daughter – it would have brought us some comfort during that hard time. We would have had a better understanding about how our daughter found herself making wrong choices. We continue to support "True Love Waits." We do not condone sexual relationships prior to marriage.

I personally took our daughter to the clinic. She had been having nausea, but attributed it to a possible sinus drainage problem. I was pretty certain that she was pregnant but had brought it up only once. When I found out that she was pregnant, I felt the joy of the Lord leave my soul. I could not sing the hymns anymore. I had a tough time facing anyone who knew the situation. In fact, I stayed in my room at school during the lunch breaks because I didn't want anyone to know. Satan tried to tell me that my prayers for my daughter were not answered. He tried to establish doubt in my heart concerning my prayer life. This was the toughest valley I had ever been through.

The only thing I knew to do was to fast and pray. For two weeks, I fasted two meals a day and spent about three hours in prayer each day. I went to the church after school when I knew no one would be there – two of those hours were spent at the church altar. I was determined that I would not give up on this. By this time in my life, I had never ceased having conversations with God. I knew He was there, but I wasn't sure about my Christian experience. Was I a total failure? Had all my work for God's kingdom been in vain? Why did this have to happen? Did I have a future left for me? I wasn't sure if I could face any congregation as a pastor's wife. I did not want to lose my joy, nor did I want my daughter to lose out on her faith, her joy, and her future. I had prayed for my daughter's future since she was a little girl. I had asked God to provide a very special husband for her just as He had provided for me. In fact, I had gone so far as to ask for Christian grandparents for our children's future children. So, where does "I'm okay, I'm all right" fit in here? From my perspective at the time, it definitely did not fit. We needed help beyond our abilities.

We found a Christian psychologist. Fortunately, our appointments were covered by my health insurance policy. Thank God for that. She worked with our daughter separately, with the three of us, and with my husband and me. In working with her, I saw a missing link. For even though she was a Christian psychologist, she never prayed with us or read scripture. She didn't because that was not a part of her practice; I wanted more for our daughter. I contacted Focus on the Family and found a Christian counselor who was on staff with her church. Her service was not covered by insurance. We never regretted paying for the sessions they spent together. She worked well with our daughter. As it turned out, the counselor had grown up in a parsonage, too. Not only did God help us find someone who could just sit and talk with our daughter, but also He had someone in place who could relate to several issues. He had someone in place who would read the Bible and pray with our daughter. I wanted our daughter to face this with confidence in God as her redeemer. I believed in our daughter's potential. I knew that she loved God.

I knew that she did not want to let any of us down. Some would say, "Wasn't your Christian faith enough to get you through this?" I believe God gave us Christian psychologists and counselors to help us understand our situations when we couldn't put all the pieces together down here on earth. I am confident those two individuals helped us to process all of this. We praise God for a positive outcome. Our faith in God never faltered.

Our son was home at the time. He was attending New Mexico State University. He knew that I was having a tough time. He got in my face and reminded me that we believe in a Redeemer! Praise the Lord! Simply put, our son wanted me to hold on to what we had practiced in our ministry. WOW! What an eye opener when I needed it. You might ask, did you reach the point in which you could say, "It's okay, I'm all right." Yes, I did. I was not willing to let Satan win. The hours I spent praying lifted my burden. The time we spent with the psychologist helped us. For in the beginning, I questioned myself as a parent. I experienced several emotions during this time. One was guilt, and others included anger and depression. I kept asking myself, "Where did I go wrong?"

It was in my questioning and my prayer time that God spoke to me. He helped me to see that I had done everything I could to try to prepare our daughter for these years. His question to me was, "What if she had gotten pregnant and you hadn't exposed her to the truth?" True love does wait. Then you would be carrying around a lot more feeling of guilt. You would have had a heavier burden. Wow! God helped me to realize that we had provided a foundation, a foundation that in later years would prove valuable in her life.

The psychologist also helped us to realize that a sixteen-year old makes most choices on his/her own. Just as our son had made choices, our daughter, too, had made choices. I finally reached a place where I could say, "It's okay, I'm all right." I could say that because I knew that we had surrendered it to God. He held the future. Reality said that our daughter would graduate from high school as a teen-age mom. She was given the choice of attending an alternative high school or continuing at the one she was attending. She chose a harder route. She faced her peers and her teachers by continuing at the high school she was attending. We were so very proud of her courageous choice.

That summer before her senior year, she and I attended a Women of Faith conference. The theme was "Bring Back the Joy." What an appropriate one for us to attend. We cried together, and we laughed together. It was a healing time for both of us. The bond between my daughter and me grew stronger. We left the conference with more confidence in the future.

We all knew that our daughter would never live in a college dormitory. She chose to give birth to her child. She also turned down the idea of adoption. She was approached by three different families. It would have made it easier to live in a dorm had she chosen to give the baby up for adoption. After she made that choice, God assured me that those families would have a child. I received a call from one of the ladies whose daughter could not have children. She called me so excited that her daughter found out that she was pregnant. Her daughter had a healthy baby. I later heard from the other families, and they did become parents. Knowing that she chose to keep the baby, we serve a gracious God. God did give her the desire of her heart. She had always wanted to attend Southern Nazarene University located in Bethany, Oklahoma. As it turned out, my husband was accepted to Oklahoma University Graduate School. At that time there were only six graduate teaching assistantships open. He was given one of them. This was in order to fulfill a second call on his life. When he was called into ministry, he also felt called to teach in higher education. He could complete a doctoral program with an emphasis in Health Communication, and our daughter would be able to attend the university of her choice. In all things God is at work when we put our complete trust in Him. Not only was I happy for my husband, but also I was happy for my daughter.

CHAPTER 12

God's Resources/God's Provisions Provide Again

When we moved to Oklahoma, we chose to live close to Southern Nazarene University. It made a longer commute for my husband and me. We both drove to Norman, Oklahoma, he for graduate school and I to teach in an elementary school. It was a shorter commute for our daughter, and we were able to get our granddaughter into a Christian daycare. She was about nine months old when she had to experience a daycare environment. Up until that point, we had been able to juggle schedules so that she could stay at home. She had some great years at that daycare all the way through her Pre-K years.

While our daughter got to attend the university of her choice, she and her daughter lived with us. She graduated with a degree in history and secondary education. For ten years she taught social studies in the seventh and eighth grade. Now she is a children's pastor. While she was in college, she got involved with the college and career group at our church. She sang in an ensemble and helped with Vacation Bible School, Caravan scouting, and the church nursery. During that time she met a wonderful young man. After dating for three years, they were married. In the wedding ceremony, he presented a ring to our granddaughter She calls him, "Dad." He officially adopted our granddaughter three years later at a time when they could financially afford it. We couldn't have been happier for our daughter and granddaughter.

CHAPTER 13

Reassurance/ Preparing for the Future/Resting on God's Promises

After the events we had gone through, some of our friends said, "You've had enough on your plate." But life teaches that as long as we are here, we may find ourselves with trials. It is how we get through them that make the difference in our lives.

While we were in Oklahoma, our son married a young woman he had met while working for Golden Bell, a Christian camping facility. Just a day after their first anniversary, a little baby girl was born. We were blessed with two granddaughters who had Christian grandparents on both sides of the family. What a blessing and an answer to prayer.

While we were still living in Oklahoma, our son informed us that he had enlisted in the military. Before our son told us, God spoke to my heart while I was driving home from school and informed me that our son had enlisted in the military. He let me know that I needed to prepare my heart. This was in November just after 9/11. We brought our son up to be patriotic. He even played army and dressed up in army outfits. But he told us as he got older that his dream was not to join the army unless someone attacked or invaded our country. When our son told us he had enlisted, he was not surprised that I didn't try to talk him out of it. When I informed him of how I knew; his words were, "I shouldn't be surprised that

God told you." I told him that when God told me I knew then that it would be okay. OKAY? Yes, because God was preparing me for this part of the journey. Our son enlisted during a time that I feared would bring him directly into war.

Although our son did not want to "grow up to be a soldier," he answered the call as did many other men and women during that time. He served three tours in Iraq. God gave me a promise that as He was with Daniel, with the three Hebrew children, and with David, He would be with my son. I rested on that promise many times. I really stayed on my knees in prayer. One of the many blessings of being a member of the family of God is the tremendous amount of prayer support received from fellow believers. I drew strength knowing that he had many people praying for him and those who were there with him.

After our son got home from his second tour, he shared his experiences with us. I am glad that I did not know all the details until then. Once a mortar landed by him but did not go off. Once he was running through a firefight with bullets going all around him. He came home untouched. In fact, the first time he went, his platoon was the only one without a purple heart. There were a total of four preacher's kids in his group. None of them knew that until they got to Iraq. What a great God we serve! Our son spoke of the many times that he was asked to pray with one of the guys with whom he was serving in Iraq. They knew about his Christian testimony. They also knew that he had much prayer surrounding him. In fact, one of the ladies in my mother's church told her that every day she prayed for an angel to watch over our son. I know that angel had to have shown up a lot.

Our son enlisted for a total of four years. It was during his second tour that my husband had a hemorrhagic stroke. This added more to our plate. Was I okay at the time of this stroke? Quite frankly, I was not. My son was in Iraq, and my daughter and her family lived fourteen hours away. But I found a place of prayer to pray and shed tears where my husband could not see me. I did not want him to know just how concerned I was. It took several tests before the doctors could come to any conclusions about what had transpired, and I was very frightened. One more time, though, the family of God surrounded us with prayer. Our families, friends from our high school days, our undergraduate days, and our graduate school days prayed for us. Friends from the churches where we grew up, friends from the churches we pastored, and friends from the church we were attending at that time prayed for us. Again we were very fortunate, and the Lord answered prayers. My husband came out of the stroke well. He spent only the better part of a week in the hospital. It took several tests before they could come to any conclusion as to what had transpired. I was very concerned and very frightened.

CHAPTER 14
God's Resources/Available Again/Healing

Surely we were finished being challenged for a while – at least I hoped so. After all, as I mentioned earlier, I always have goals and plans. Those plans definitely did not include my personal struggle with cancer.

As you know from what I have already written in my story, we are firm believers in healing granted through prayer and anointing. Before my cancer, I had come through five surgeries and two experiences with hospitalization due to blood clots. I was present when my grandmother was healed in her eighties. My husband and my brother-in law, who are ordained ministers, anointed my grandmother, and we gathered around her with prayer. She lived eleven years past the time the doctors expected her to live. Her personal physician and her cardiologist said that she was a walking miracle.

In addition to those healings, other examples abounded of God's healing touch. God touched our son when he was an infant. He was running a fever of 104 degrees. We had given him Tylenol and a lukewarm bath, but the fever continued. Even though we had insurance, we did not want to go to the emergency room due to a high deductible amount. Acute care clinics didn't exist at that time and, because it was night time, even if they did, they wouldn't have been open. In our desperation we decided for my husband to anoint him. Thank God, the fever left. God also touched my niece when she was a little girl. My sister called me, and we all made it a matter of prayer. She was healed.

My husband, Ken, has experienced healing. We were pastoring in Oklahoma when an ENT specialist told him that the nodules on his vocal chords looked malignant. We did what we knew to do: We turned to God in prayer and conversation. My husband went through a tough time. His voice was his only means of making a living for his family. He had a double call in his life. As I mentioned earlier, one was to preach and the other was to teach at the college level. He hadn't even had a chance to pursue his call to teach. So, could it be that malignancy would cut it short? Ken wasn't quite sure what was ahead. His conversation with God involved some questioning. What purpose would malignancy serve? After the surgery, the surgeon expressed with surprise that the nodules were benign. That was great news to our hearts. God truly touched Ken. There was no doubt in our minds. Through this experience, he did learn how to preach without overwhelming his vocal chords. In order for that to be accomplished, he spent some time in voice therapy. So, why did my husband have a stroke years later after experiencing God's healing on his vocal chords? We don't know, but the severity of that stroke was not as bad as it could have been. God was working on my husband's behalf.

These times of healing strengthened our resolve, but our faith was to be challenged again. My diagnosis of cancer came after his stroke. How could I say, "It's okay, I'm all right?" I had not experienced healing to the point of the mass in my chest wall being benign. Why did God answer the prayer for my husband's healing and not mine? As a word of encouragement, our son came up to me in the hospital and whispered, "If God can bring me home from Iraq, He can get you through this." Once again God used our son to remind me of the foundation we had established with our children. That touched my heart.

My journey through the experience of chemotherapy had its moments or, should I say, sometimes its days? I had told God long before this happened that if I ended up with cancer I did not want to have to go through being constantly nauseated. He granted my prayers. I had nausea only twice. I did have mouth sores. I did lose my hair. I did have days with no strength to get out of bed. There is no way I could have had peace in my heart except through prayer and time spent in God's word. The added support that I needed came through my family, my colleagues from the schools where I was teaching, and the family of God. My mom and my sisters were here to help me with the recovery period associated with the surgery. My middle sister, our daughter, and my husband took turns sitting with me during my chemotherapy treatments. Mine took a total of 6 ½ hours each time it was administered. I joked with the nurses that my insurance company and I must be paying rent because I was in there longer than anyone else each time I came.

I can't count the number of times that my name was lifted up in prayer. I have a special box set aside for the cards and letters that I received during that time. Plus, the meals and gift cards for meals we received made our days easier.

I am one of the fortunate ones that had to have only six treatment sessions. An additional CT-scan was done after my surgery, and it revealed that there was a growth in my throat area. That required a series of steroid tablets after each chemo treatment. We received the profoundly good news that the bone marrow test indicated that there was no cancer present. The PET scan revealed I was affected with the cancer only in the areas already found. Praise God! I can thank God for taking care of that for me. When were those areas of my body protected? We will never know for certain, but I believe that, when I was anointed, God took care of them. As I mentioned earlier, during my treatment I did experience a couple of days of nausea. I lost my appetite. It seemed as if nearly everything tasted like metal. I had days of exhaustion to the point of not getting out of bed. That was mainly because my white cell count had dropped to .5 on a scale that should have shown at least 4.3.

After the fourth treatment, a CT-scan was done to check the

progress of the chemotherapy. A blood clot was found in my lung. Talk about God's intervention – I spent only six days in the hospital with that. Once again, it is miraculous how God works. I had no idea that I had a blood clot in my lung, and I could have died from that. I learned that sometimes cancer patients develop blood clots. Because this was my third experience with clots, I now have a filter in my veins to catch any that might develop. It will prevent them from traveling to my heart or my lungs. I will be on blood thinners for the rest of my life. It seems that in spite of those things, God had other plans for me.

God knows me well. He had all things worked out ahead of time. I had purchased salary protection insurance, so I did not have to worry about whether or not I could make it to work. I did not have to worry about all the germs I would encounter teaching kindergarten through second-grade students. That was a great gift.

The thing I missed the most was getting to attend church. My youngest sister whose daughter had leukemia explained to me that it was vital to protect myself from all contacts that could expose me to germs. Her daughter underwent lengthy chemo treatments. She spent additional time in public and ended up sick in the hospital due to viruses, etc., to which she was exposed. Praise God, at this writing, she has been cancer-free for fourteen years. I spent five months listening to preaching on the television and listening to our church service on the radio. Thank goodness for those means of communication.

Were my days of "It's okay, I'm all right" over? No, a month after my diagnosis, my middle sister learned that she had breast cancer. Once again, God interceded on behalf of our family. Interceded? Yes, he did. Her cancer was found in stage one. She had a mammogram done after she and her husband moved to Kansas to pastor a church there. She told me that it was because of my diagnosis and the fact that they had insurance that she had a mammogram done. She lived forty-five minutes from where we lived. She had to undergo only radiation. The malignancy was just one centimeter in size, and it was encased by fibers that measured seven centimeters; therefore, it did not move to any other place in her body. With her lymph nodes all clear, her prognosis was good. She received services in the same cancer center that I did. We lived close enough to each other to share in this experience. Believe it or not, we laughed and rejoiced at the fact that our mother, who was seventy-six at that time, was the one to take care of us. We thought by then that the roles might be reversed. It was good to have someone to cry and laugh with during those times. Laughter is indeed a medicine. Our attitude is so important when reflecting upon life's issues.

So cancer impacted three sisters, two of us personally and one through her daughter. People have told us that our attitudes make a difference. I am convinced of that. I will always be eternally grateful for the difference God has made in my journey.

That is the only way that any of us have been able to smile. We have a Friend who is in control.

I know if I been given a different diagnosis it would have been a lot harder to smile. God did answer the prayer of my small group, the prayer for healing. God did work through anointing. I had to undergo only six treatments. The last PET scan results were negative. That meant that the chemo worked well, and no cancer was present. I have a voice and an opportunity to praise God. I no longer have to struggle for breath support. God used the chemotherapy to bring about my healing. I returned to work in the fall, and I returned to church on a regular basis.

I want to be able to pass our special heritage down to other generations. This is one of the motivating reasons why I am writing this. I found a long time ago that the most important priority in my life is the salvation of our family. If I had been told that I only had a few months or days left, I could have left this world knowing that my family was secure.

CHAPTER 15
God's Reassurance/ Trust Him in All Things

Had our son's or daughter's families not been serving God, I would not have been able to say, "It's okay, I'm all right." But they were!

The story of our journey continued. I did return to teaching. In fact, I was having the best year of my teaching career. I had helped the school district establish a new program in special education. All things were going well; however, I realized more and more that I was having trouble breathing. I just couldn't get enough breath support. I also found myself without enough energy. In February, I thought I was coming down with bronchitis. I was approaching another three-month check-up. By now, I had been seeing a cardiologist because the chemo had created a fast heart rate. The cardiologist had ordered some lab work. On the day that I had my check-up with the oncologist, I took care of getting the additional lab on my blood count. I thought I could go back to school and finish the day, but I was exhausted. When I went home, I laid down. Two hours after the results from the lab were in, I got a call from my cardiologist. He informed me that the report did not look good. He said he wanted me to meet him at the hospital, not through the ER, but through admissions to be checked in. Once again, I didn't hesitate.

I was admitted to the hospital. Immediately following that, the doctor came to my room and informed my husband and me that I had 95 % congestive heart failure. After that discussion with my doctor, I saw a continuous gold light in the shape of a cone streaming into the room. There was only a section left without the gold. It was not due to sunlight coming in…the color was indescribable… such a beautiful gold. I asked God if this meant that I was dying. Apparently, I was close to leaving this world. When the doctors gave us the report, I thought to myself, "In other words, I am barely alive." Once again, God had interceded in my life. At this point, I told God that I really didn't want to add another chapter to my story. (Imagine my smiling at that statement because I was just trying to joke a little at my circumstance.) I am so thankful that the God I serve knows me well. Had I not had the additional blood tests done, we would not have found the problem in time to save my life.

It's okay, I'm all right? Our son was in Iraq for a third time. I believe that God protected my life because of how difficult it would have been for our son to lose me at that point in his life. To me, I serve such a wonderful God that He cares about every area of our lives. I don't hesitate to think that way. It reminded me of an earlier time when I asked God to allow my grandfather's passing to happen at a time when we could be present. My grandfather appeared to be terminal. It was over the Christmas holidays, and we were all present. It was bitterly cold and the ground was covered with ice. During those years we were living in New Mexico, and I couldn't make the long journey very many times during the school year. As it turned out, my grandfather did pass away while we were on Christmas vacation, and we were all there.

Perhaps some people would think that I take too many things for granted about God's intercession, but I don't think so, not after serving Him for all these years. He knows us better than we know ourselves. As for my family and me, we believe in a gracious and merciful God. We have seen Him at work in our lives. I do not believe that was a selfish prayer about the timing of my grandfather's passing. I don't think God did either. If he could bring Lazarus back from the dead, he could take my grandfather on to Heaven when we all could be there to share in our grief and celebrate my grandfather's homegoing to Heaven. God knows what we can endure. In the same way, I believe God knew what our son could endure and what I could endure, and my life was spared.

Again, you might say, "gracious?" After all, I had 95% heart failure. My son went to Iraq a third time. But amid all of what happened up to that point, I still trusted God as Lord of my life. There were still long days of endurance. There were days when I longed for the promises of God. My story was still being written. At the time that I wrote this part of my story, I found myself in a situation where my heart was only functioning at 50% capacity. I have permanent damage to my left ventricle, so I had to go to rehab and do exercises to strengthen it. I had to take five different heart meds and have regular check-ups. I wrote this part of my story while I was sitting at home, for I wasn't teaching anymore. Before I left the hospital, the doctors told me that I could not return to work. In other words, I had a choice of returning to teaching or living long enough to see my granddaughters (who were five and eight at the time), and any other grandchildren who would be a part of our family, grow up. It didn't take me long to make my choice. Naturally, I chose life. That was not exactly how I had planned to live out my life. I still wanted to be teaching special needs children. I enjoyed helping children, teachers, and families. Fortunately, God gave me the insight to keep my disability insurance.

CHAPTER 16
Regroup/Trusting God's Provisions/Decisions

How did "it's okay, I'm all right" fit in now? I went through a personal grieving period when I had to give up teaching. A portion of my identity had been taken away. However, in spite of it all, I found myself being very grateful that my lack of energy was due to a physical problem and not that I was "just getting old." My prayer was that God would once again show me what He needed me to do with my life. I found myself without all the answers. Where do we go from here? By the end of the semester, my husband's career changed again. We moved back to Oklahoma. He continued being a professor, just for a different university. We continued to be actively involved in a church. I took every opportunity to praise the Lord and give Him honor and glory. Once more He kept me alive to continue serving Him. It was during that particular time that I did find some time to write more of our story.

A wonderful surprise was that I added more to my story. At the end of December 2007, I had an ultrasound of the heart procedure. The doctor informed me that my heart was pumping at the rate it should be. Naturally I asked him if that meant that I could return to teaching. His response was, "Yes, part-time for a while, and, if all goes well, then you can return for full-time." The doctor told me that my heart's strength and function returned due to medication, rehab exercises, and rest. I added the words, "and God's touch." The prayers for healing had been heard once again. My family and I don't mind making that statement.

I would end this part of our story by returning to Psalm 34:4-22 (NIV):

> I sought the Lord, and he answered me;
> he delivered me from all my fears.
> Those who look to him are radiant;
> their faces are never covered with shame.
> This poor man called, and the Lord heard him;
> he saved him out of all his troubles.
> The angel of the Lord encamps around those who
> fear him, and he delivers them.
>
> Taste and see that the Lord is good;
> blessed is the man who takes refuge in him.
> Fear the Lord, you his holy people,
> for those who fear him lack nothing.
> The lions may grow weak and hungry,
> but those who seek the Lord lack no good thing.
> Come, my children, listen to me;
> I will teach you the fear of the Lord.
> Whoever of you loves life
> and desires to see many good days,
> keep your tongue from evil
> and your lips from speaking lies.
> Turn from evil and do good;
> seek peace and pursue it.
>
> The eyes of the Lord are on the righteous,
> and his ears are attentive to their cry;
> but the face of the Lord is against those who do evil,
> to blot out their name from the earth.

The righteous cry out, and the Lord hears them;
he delivers them from all their troubles.
The Lord is close to the brokenhearted
and saves those who are crushed in spirit.

The righteous person may have many troubles,
but the Lord delivers him from them all;
he protects all his bones,
not one of them will be broken.

Evil will slay the wicked;
the foes of the righteous will be condemned.
The Lord will rescue his servants;
no one who takes refuge in him will be condemned.

May summertime and sunshine be found in your heart. Take refuge
in the Lord.

Isn't it amazing that He gave us His son?
Isn't it amazing that He showed us His love?
Isn't it amazing that He takes us back?
Isn't it amazing what a Father will do?
I am amazed with each new day.
I am amazed at what grace will do.
And I am amazed that He loved me still.

Isn't it amazing?
Isn't it amazing?

I am amazed by His glory and grace.
I am amazed by His hope and His love.
Of God's gifts from above
I stand amazed.
                              K. Brown II

Our son wrote those verses just after I was declared cancer free and he had made it back to America one more time. He pointed out to me, "Mom, you didn't need to write another chapter in your story." I hadn't planned on it either, but, as we all know, life happens. That chapter of my life certainly was one of the most difficult of all. You might say, "How can it be the most difficult when you and your family made it through so many things?" My entire story has been focused on "It's okay, I'm all right."

CHAPTER 17
Blessed Assurance/ God Showed Up Again/Respond to His Leadership

I find myself adding another chapter in my life – this one, one for which I had no time to think about what I was going to experience. My life was spared one more time. The survival rate for what I was about to go through is 2-5%. I had just come through another surgery to repair a hernia, and all went well, we thought. After all... just one more surgery, and this one was supposed to have pretty good success rates. I had already had this done before. One month and two days after that surgery, I lost my entire colon. The colon had expanded to the point that it became septic, and the poison from it was seeping into my major organs and my bloodstream. The antibiotic that I had been given after the surgery mixed with the bacteria in my colon, and I experienced what is known in medical terms as C-diff.

I am alive today because our son heard the voice of God speaking to him. It wasn't the first time He spoke to him. After he had been out of the Army for a while, he re-enlisted, and he went to Iraq one more time. It was during that time that he heard God tell him to sit down. God spoke to him using military lingo. Our son radioed ahead to see if the First Sergeant had called him to order him to sit down. The answer was, "No." He asked the soldiers in the vehicle with him if they told him to sit down. "No." He was in the lead vehicle looking for IEDs on the road. He had no place to sit down, but he got down. He knew that is must be God speaking to him. After he sat down, a rocket-propelled grenade flew through the spot where he had been standing. God protected him and kept him alive. God was keeping the promise He had given me when my son enlisted. Prior to his leaving Iraq, the vehicle he was in went over an IED. Even though his vehicle went airborne, he was blessed in that the only thing he went through was a concussion. He was hospitalized for a week, and he ended up with a traumatic brain injury. That qualified him to be a recipient of a purple heart. He has that in a special place. Like many of his "brothers" in service to this country, he did not feel worthy of the award. His injury at the time did not render him incapable of continuing his service in the Army, but it did change his orders.

After Iraq, our son was sent to Korea for a period of three years. He worked his way up to achieve the rank of a Level 4 instructor in combatants. He will say that it helped a lot with his PTSD. After he left Korea, he spent his last months left in the military in the states. While he was in Korea, his wife and daughter were able to join him there. During that time they were there, they had a little boy born prematurely. He ended up with a hernia. They were sent to a hospital where most of the people spoke Korean. They had to wait in line to be served. Our son called us so very concerned. They were told that if their son didn't get help, he might not live. So, as we always have done, our family went to prayer. Our son looked up, and two Korean ladies approached him. They asked him what was wrong because they saw him crying. Those ladies told him they were Christians. One spoke these words in broken English: "I'll go get you some help, and, while I am gone, can my friend pray with you?" Within just a few minutes, a surgeon came. He placed his hands on our little grandson and moved the hernia out of the way. They don't do surgery on infants in Korea until they are six months old. God sent some very special angels that day. After the surgeon finished, the ladies left and they never saw them again. The scriptures refer to the fact that we sometime have angels attend to us. That day our new little grandson and his family did!

I've learned that if God ever places something on our hearts, such as making a phone call, we need to do it. God spoke to our son a second time, and I'm thankful he responded. It was late one Sunday afternoon after our son was back in the states that he felt he should call me because He heard the same voice as in Iraq, only this time he heard, "Call your mom." So he called me. After talking to me, he could tell that I was not well. In fact, he said that he thought I sounded like my grandmother. I was so very ill. My husband had offered to take me to the doctor, but I told him, "I'll get better tomorrow. I probably have a virus." Hmmm, how many times have we thought that kind of thing, it will be better tomorrow? My son told me to give the phone to my husband. He told my husband to get me to an ER. Thankfully, he did.

I do not remember riding in the car to the ER. I do not remember those doctors or nurses. I do not even remember riding in an ambulance to Mercy Hospital in Oklahoma City. Fortunately, the ER doctors in local hospital knew my case was more than they could handle.

I Thessalonians 5:16-17, 23-24

Be joyful always; pray continually; give thanks in all circumstances, for this is God's will for you in Christ Jesus.

Do not put out the Spirit's fire; do not treat prophecies with contempt. Test everything. Hold on to the good. Avoid every kind of evil.

May God himself the God of peace, sanctify you through and through. May your whole spirit soul and body be kept blameless at the coming of our Lord Jesus Christ. The one who calls you is faithful and he will do it.

I woke up after the emergency surgery for removing my colon had happened and found out that I had just spent 12 days in an ICU unit. I don't remember anything about the ICU experience. They say that when people are on life support systems, the medications they are given keep patients pretty much subdued so that they won't fight the ventilator or any other equipment being used. I also had to receive dialysis. I'm glad that I have no memory of those things. They tell me that dialysis is very rough on the body. God spared me of having to be alert enough to endure that. My husband, our son and daughter and their families, my sisters, my parents, my nieces, and my nephews do remember those days. It is more difficult for the family who waits patiently for good news concerning the loved one in the ICU unit, especially if they watch family after family lose their loved ones. I was told by more than one person that our daughter spent part of her time praying with families in the ICU who were not our family members. I believe that He needed our daughter to be there to represent Him to those families who were needing someone to pray for them. The question is, "Why was my life spared one more time?"

Our family watched families cry with grief. Jesus' mother and those who watched Him die were crying with grief. He had told them He would raise the temple in three days. How??? Building the temple took a long time. He was talking about a different temple. He is risen indeed! The temple He referred to was His life. For those who serve Jesus, there is the promise of a new life in Heaven when we leave this earth in death. For those who don't have a relationship with Him, it will be a different kind of eternity.

I was prepared to meet God in eternity, but my family, as all families, wanted to have me here for more time spent together. My son and daughter enjoyed telling me that they saw a little "light at the end of the tunnel" when I tried to get the ventilator out of my mouth. Apparently, they saw me scoot down in the bed, reach over, and try to take the ventilator out of my mouth. We laugh about that now, but to them it represented my struggle to fight that foreign object in my mouth. That meant signs of life. Many people have told me that I have a lot of fight in my system. I believe is an inherited trait from my mom's family. My mom's mom lived to be 91. She fought many physical battles but always had a sweet spirit and trusted Jesus. My mom came through the many things she faced. She, too, trusted in Jesus. Just recently, my aunt told someone about me: "That fighting spirit is what helped her fight the physical battles that she has fought." God knew me in my mother's womb. God provided that fighting spirit for me as I've gone through these many struggles.

My son told me that he went to the chapel and prayed for me. He heard God say,

> "It's in my hands." This time it was a softer, sweeter voice. Now the job for our son was to trust God for the outcome. My heart crashed three times when the only way they could get a blood pressure reading or pulse was to use the ultra sound. The doctors told my family to prepare for the end. So my struggling with that ventilator was truly a joyous experience. They could smile again.

At that point the nursing staff put restraints on my arms so that I could not remove the ventilator. (I don't blame them.) I have claustrophobia, and, even in my semi-conscious state, I did not like those restraints. I do remember rolling over to one side and using my right hand to get the restraint off my left hand. I couldn't roll over to get the other one off of my right hand, so I used the nurse call button. Guess what she did. She did not help me get the right one off; in fact, she placed the left one on again. ☺

I spent a total of twenty-four days in the hospital. The restraints were finally taken off, and I was given a chance to try getting out of bed holding onto a walker. I worked so hard to stand with the walker because I knew it meant that I could leave the hospital if I could successfully use a walker. I was so glad when I finally got to leave the hospital, even if it was in a wheel chair that I would use for quite a while.

CHAPTER 18
Regrouping/God Are You Sure About This?

The next phase was spending time in a nursing home facility to get my motor skills working again. That truly was a humbling experience. I was totally dependent on help getting out of bed and getting to the bathroom. I had to learn how to become mobile using a wheelchair or a walker. After all of the prior surgeries, I was able to walk. They told me that having spent so much time in the ICU and the other unit caused my body to atrophy. In other words, I didn't have much muscle ability in my body. It was so frustrating to me that one day I spent awhile figuring out how to get to the bathroom using the wheelchair. I wasn't patient enough to wait for a nurse to walk me to the bathroom. I ended up being trapped in there. After successfully navigating my way into the bathroom I couldn't get the door open to leave the bathroom. My being a touch claustrophobic didn't help either. No one answered my signal light from within that bathroom for twenty minutes. I began to try to figure out how I would get out if no one responded. At that point I was dependent on someone to teach me how to take care of my ileostomy bag, too. ☹ I am certain that I had a conversation with God about my being trapped, and His response was not one of condemnation but one of reminding me that I was blessed just to be breathing. He also reminded me to be grateful for that button in the bathroom.☺

Fortunately, before I left the skilled nursing home facility, God sent a Christian young lady who had moved to America from

Ghana. She was one of the certified nursing assistants. She was very fluent in English. She became one of the bright lights during the days and nights when no one else was there. More humbling was when I finally got to eat in the dining room. Wow. There were people who were much worse off than I. Some of them never had anyone come to visit them. During my stay in the hospital and my time in the nursing home, I had many visitors who made my days brighter. My nieces, who lived in the OKC area, came to the hospital to see me as often as they could. Many of our church family friends plus one of my former principals helped me get my tray into a position where I could eat. My husband still had teaching responsibilities, so he couldn't come and spend his day with me, but I also had visits from my friends on the faculty where I was currently teaching come to visit me.

Finally, there came a day when I was allowed to return home. After I came home, I must admit there were days of ups and downs. I had appointments with all of my specialists once I got home. Therapists and nurses made visits to our home. One specifically told me that I needed to get counseling from a counselor. Fortunately, I knew a Christian counselor. She was able to fit me into her schedule. I lived with the "if only" complex. Have you ever experienced that? I blamed myself for having the surgery to correct my hernia. I thought if I had not had the surgery I might not have gotten the C-diff. She helped me to realize that we can't live that way. I knew that but I had given myself permission to have a "pity party" of the "if only" kind. My digestive disease specialist told me that if I hadn't gotten that hernia repaired, I might have found myself bleeding to death or I might have had a strangled colon, which would have led to a surgery anyway. In fact, just two months after I got home, I had a day of what I thought was discouragement. I had been up all night dealing with pain associated with my intestinal track (what was left of it). I had to check every hour. I was beginning to tire of having to choose foods that wouldn't block up the digestive system. Seems pretty petty? I know there are so many people who never know if they will even have a next meal.

I was depressed. Finally, at about 4 o'clock in the afternoon, I knew I needed to stop my little "pity party" and kneel and pray. In my conversation with God, He said, "You know what you need to do." I picked up my Bible and read from Deuteronomy 3 and 4. Those chapters specifically pointed out the need to have mothers teach their children and grandchildren about God. I enjoy being with my family so much, and I'm glad I have more time to share the love of Jesus with my family. Thank you, God, for sparing my life.

Our daughter had a four-year-old son at that time. He kept his mom, dad, and sister very busy. It was always exciting to talk to him on the phone. It was even better to hear his version of what he was learning in church. He told his children's director at the church that Jesus died for his sins, his dad's, his mom's, his sister's, his grandparents', and his Spiderman's, Batman's, and his Ironman's at home. Those little grandsons were just beginning to become acquainted with their grandmother. My heart's desire still is that they, too, will learn to love Jesus in the same way in which I do.

After our oldest granddaughter spent most of the summer with us that year, we had to take her back to her home to help with Vacation Bible School. She was such a blessing helping me. So were her mom and their family. Our son and his family came that summer, too. I am grateful that our family is so close in our relationships, especially considering what we went through in our children's teen years. What could have been destroyed was redeemed through God's mercy and grace.

We got to our daughter's home in time to be in church with her and her family. That Sunday the pastor preached an excellent message on being a born again Christian totally committed to the Lord Jesus Christ. In other words, a person can't be a productive Christian with one foot in the Kingdom of God and one foot hanging on the fence of where the world would like for him or her to be. It is easier for God to intercede when one is totally open to His leadership.

CHAPTER 19
Regrouping/Accepting God's Plan/His Perfect Will

As we drove home down the road through west Texas, I saw fertile crops on one side of the road and nothing fertile on the other side. I saw irrigation systems on one side and no sign of any systems on the other side. As recorded in the scripture, "It is hard for seed to grow on dry ground." So much of my energy had been spent on just trying to reach some kind of "normal" that I found myself thirsty for fellowship with God. It reminded me of a dream I had when I woke up in the hospital just after those days in the ICU. In the dream I was an observer in what seemed to be a dark hole. It was a haunting dream. There was a voice that spoke to a young lady in that dark hole. She had no way out. There wasn't a rock wall available nor a ladder. She was told that she would spend her life in the hole with eternal darkness because she never stayed true to her life with Christ. She had chosen a different lifestyle. She would have to spend eternity in darkness. I don't know about you, but I hate being in the dark. I even have night-lights in our house. I woke up almost in a panic attack because it was so dark and empty in that dream.

I believe there are a lot of people today who still live in that darkness. They try all different means available to them to fill that gap in their lives. Jesus is the only one who can fill that void in their lives.

When I finally woke up from the medical coma, I was a little bit confused. I asked my sister if I were still alive. That was a strange question because there certainly was not a brilliant light in the room, and I couldn't see streets of gold or hear a choir of saints singing praises to God. She happily told me, "Yes." She tells me my first response was, "Oh, good, we have time to tell more people we need to tell them they need to accept Jesus as their Savior. They need forgiveness of their sins so they can go to Heaven." That was not just a passing thought. I have been concerned for those who do not have Christ in their lives ever since I felt God's call on my life at age nine. That dream I had was just a glimpse of what total darkness will be like. Those who are not Christians are living without the "Light of the World," Jesus Christ. I serve Him not just because of the promise of Heaven, but because He first loved me. He is the reason that I can still say those words, "It is okay, I'm all right."

From what I have written in my story, it is clear that I believe in the power of prayer. God has spoken to me about the fact that I need to pray more than ever before. (At this point, I have more time.) At the very time that God spoke to me about prayer, He also spoke to me about pursuing a minister's license. After all, I had been a special speaker at Mother's Day services, a guest speaker for local congregations, and a speaker for Ladies' Ministries luncheons/ retreats. My conversation with God went something like this: "I thought I was finished with studying anything except for Children's Bible study and the Wednesday night services. After all, I have 59 graduate hours that were very helpful in my teaching career. But, I don't know, Lord, if this sixty-two- year old brain is ready to take course work and write papers. How does this fall into the category of 'It's ok, I'm all right?' I have trusted you through many things. Are you sure you want me to do this?"

Thank goodness, God has patience, a sense of humor, and grace. He didn't reprimand me but filled me with a special assurance that one more time He would lead me on my journey in life.

During October of 2013 my husband presented me with a Local

Minister's license. At the time I didn't believe God had spoken to me about being a Senior/Lead Pastor of a church. My husband had been in full-time ministry over thirty years. We both had served in full-time children's ministry early in our lives. He had also served as an interim pastor for a few churches. I felt very comfortable letting him take the lead. My preaching once a month on Sundays was fine with me. But I entered our denomination's course of study. I completed the work and was approved by our denominational board of studies and ministry. I was ordained in April of 2018.

I want my story to serve as an encouragement to those who read it. Yes, we can have summertime in our hearts even when we feel it is like winter. When our lives are dedicated to the Lord Jesus Christ, we can reach the place where we can say, "It's okay, I'm all right."

Printed in the United States
By Bookmasters